BY KYLE BAKER

MARLOWE & COMPANY
NEW YORK

First Marlowe & Company edition, 1996

Published by
Marlowe & Company
632 Broadway, Seventh Floor
New York, NY 10012

Published by arrangement with Doubleday, a division of
Bantam Doubleday Dell Publishing Group, Inc.

Manufactured in the United States of America

Library of Congress Cataloging-in-Publication Data

Baker, Kyle.
    The Cowboy Wally Show / by Kyle Baker.
        p.   cm.
    Originally published :   New York : Doubleday, 1988.
    ISBN 1-56924-834-6
    I. Title.
PN6727.B33C6   1996   95-26353
741.5'973—dc20   CIP

QUESTIONS OR COMMENTS? Send them to Ldeneault@aol.com

Dedications:
Chapter 1 is for my parents.
Chapter 3 is for Ron Fontes
The remaining two chapters
will be auctioned off sometime
next Fall.

Acknowledgments:
I blame society.

Chapter One: The Cowboy Wally Legend

Chapter One: THE COWBOY WALLY LEGEND (documentary, 1987)

In one of the many rare interviews he has given, the legendary film star is as candid and witty as ever. With interviewer Oswald "Glassy" Stairs, Cowboy Wally traces his remarkable career from his early days as a children's show host ("COWBOY WALLY'S SHOOT 'EM UP LAUGH RIOT," 1974) to his present day variety spectaculars ("COWBOY WALLY'S ROOTIN' TOOTIN' HORN O'PLENTY All-STAR CELEBRITY HALF-TIME SHOW," 1988). A vastly entertaining film.

Whooshman–
Bicarbonate
Films
presents

a
Cowboy Wally
Film

The Cowboy Wally Legend

Cowboy Wally. A man who is the living embodiment of the American Dream. A man adored by millions.

But who is Cowboy Wally?

Who is the man who lived the Cinderella story which transformed him from an impoverished free-lance photographer to a superstar literally overnight?

On a hunch, we decided to ask him. This is his story.

We visited Cowboy Wally at his modest home in Jeepersville, North Dakota, just a few miles away from the **Cowboy Wally's Funland Amusement Park.**

Hi, I'm Oswald Stairs.

Oh, yes. "Glassy." Cowboy Wally is expecting you. I'm his butler, Carol. Follow me please.

Okay.

Wait, I messed that up. I was supposed to say, "Walk this way." He thought it would be funnier. I'm sorry.

That's Okay.

No, I messed it up. Cowboy Wally wanted to do you guys a big favor and give you a funny joke to start off your movie, and now it's ruined. I'm sorry. He's in the den. Come on. I mean, walk this way. Oh, I'm sorry.

I'd have to say that basically you're just a regular guy.

For a big star.

For a big star.

So, let's get this interview rolling, okay?

Right. Okay. Thanks. First of all, a lot of folks want to know how you got your start in show business?

Well, I used to be a free-lance photographer...

And so, anyways, one day on a whim, I introduced myself to the president of the WQZ television network, Mr. Jameson Spleen.

I showed him some pictures that I had taken of him and his thirteen-year-old niece, Stephanie.

Spleen was so impressed that he offered me ten thousand dollars cash and my own television series in exchange for the pictures and negatives.

Wow.

And the rest is history.

You must have been some photographer.

Unfortunately, I hear those pictures have since been lost.

Cowboy Wally's Shoot 'em Up Laugh Riot, 1974

Hey, hey, kiddies! It's time for **Cowboy Wally's Shoot 'em Up Laugh Riot!**

Well, we're gonna have some fun today, kiddies! Professor Gosh will be here later, and he's going to make naked ladies out of balloons! And Julie, here, and I are going to sing a duet!

But first, I wanna tell you the joke about the blind dog and the midget in the suit of armor.

After the first show aired, the network got a lot of letters from upset parents.

These parents were saying that my " lewd and rowdy manner " was not appropriate for children's programming.

The network agreed, and I was moved to prime time. Hey! Here's my manager, Sol!

Sorry I'm late! You didn't tell them anything yet, did you, Wally?

Yeah. We've been having a nice talk, Sol.

Of course! And why shouldn't you? You have nothing to hide!

Cowboy Wally and the West Pecos Mounted Armada, 1974

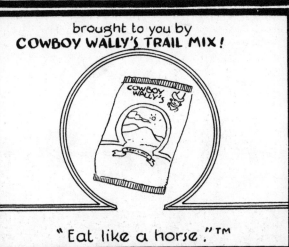

Cowboy Wally and the West Pecos Mounted Armada, 1974

The game show lasted about two weeks.

It's doing really well in syndicated reruns, though.

Then you went into film.

Yes, I produced and directed a movie. A guy had come to me with a great script called **Rothro, Lizard of Doom**.

I loved it, but I figured a lot of people would have trouble remembering the name. I know I did.

So I made a few changes, and we released the film.

Ed Smith,
Lizard of Doom
1976

Oh no. Ed Smith, Lizard of Doom, has come from a planet far beyond our solar system to devour us.

Gaze and tremble, mortals. None can escape the wrath of Ed Smith, Lizard of Doom.

EEEEEEEEEEEEEEEEE!
EEEEEEEEEEEEEEEEEE!
EEEEEEEEEEEEEEEEEE!

There must be some way to stop him, but how? HOW?

The movie didn't do too well. I think it was ahead of its time. If it had been released today, it would have been a big hit.

Tell us about "Rough-up Theater."

Oh, that was a TV project of mine. Every week, I'd present a story of real men in the Old West. It was exciting and educational.

Cowboy Wally's Rough-up Theater, 1976

Dry Falls Gulch, 1843.

Left hook, Jab.
Right cross, combination.
Uppercut.

Mister, where I come from, them's fightin' words.

...brought to you by
COWBOY WALLY'S FUNLAND™
Amusement Park
Jeepersville, N.D.

"beer and free toilets."

The show was canceled in two weeks.

But the reruns are big in France.

You've had success with your amusement park, though.

Oh yes. Cowboy Wally's Funland. It started off slowly, but now business is booming.

I think the slow start was because of all the bad press we got early on. People saying the park was too dangerous for children.

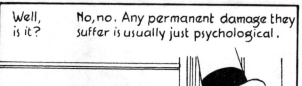

Well, is it?

No, no. Any permanent damage they suffer is usually just psychological.

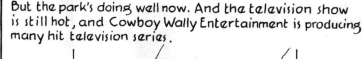

But the park's doing well now. And the television show is still hot, and Cowboy Wally Entertainment is producing many hit television series.

And I do have my own line of beef products. And, of course, the menswear, hair tonic, T-shirts, razor blades, lunch boxes, and feminine hygiene products are doing well, so I'm okay.

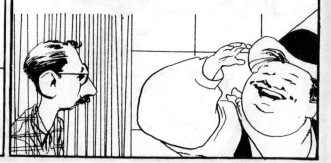

Not bad for someone who Dick Cavett once described as "the stupidest man on the face of this planet."

Stupid? I don't know the meaning of the word.

a joke.

by Cowboy Wally

CLAP CLAP CLAP CLAP CLAP CLAP CLAP CLAP CLA

Okay, so there's these two guys, right? Okay, so this one guy says to the other... oh, right, they're in a bar. Okay, so these two guys, anyway, so...

...So he says to the guy, who's black, he says to him, no, wait, he's Chinese. He says, "Hey, have you seen my mother-in-law?" No, wife...

...It's his wife, right. So he says, "Hey, have you seen my wife? And so the bartender says... no, the Jew, Chinese, the Chinese guy, he HAW HAW!

HAW... snort.
Sorry, I just remembered something funny.

From its beginnings as **Cowboy Wally's shoot 'em Up Laugh Riot** to its later incarnation as **Cowboy Wally and the West Pecos Mounted Armada** the Cowboy Wally program had been consistently strong in the ratings.

But at the start of the 1980s, it looked as though Cowboy Wally would lose everything. We asked him to recall that time.

Well, it all started with the 1979 Christmas episode. Our Christmas shows are always ratings blockbusters. And with good reason.

This one was an extravaganza. We had 8,000 cheerleaders and 100,000 balloons. During the course of the show, I was fired from a cannon 16 times. Special guests included Burt Convy, Loni Anderson, and the Living Unicorn.

We also had Amy Flaxman, the Charlene Tilton impersonator, jumping on a trampoline while juggling an orange, a bowling ball, and a waffle iron.

The highlight of the show was **Trixie's Bubble dance**.

I accompanied her by making various noises on a hot water bottle with a rubber hose until I passed out.

Truly remarkable.

Wasn't it, though. The switchboard was lit up like Times Square.

the hearings, day 4

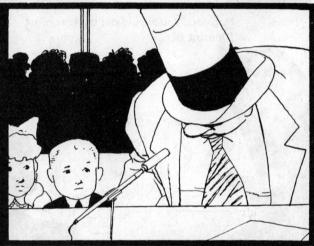

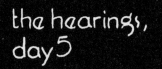

the hearings,
day 5

I would just like to say, on behalf of the committee, that we are honored that you could make it today.

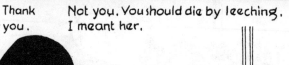

Thank you.

Not you. You should die by leeching. I meant her.

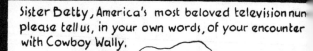

Sister Betty, America's most beloved television nun, please tell us, in your own words, of your encounter with Cowboy Wally.

Well, I was in front of the bus depot collecting for the convent...

...when that man, Cowboy Wally, passed by.

I asked him if he could spare some change, and he said "Get a job."

Senator, I think we can discount her testimony as unsubstantiated hearsay.

That was you?

Let's jump ahead a couple of years. 1985 was an important year in your life.

That's right. We started the Wally Broadcasting Network.

We had something like twenty great new shows. Lots of publicity.

WBN Promo
1985

Hey, hey, kids! It's your old pal, Cowboy Wally, inviting you to watch Sunday night's debut of the Wally Broadcasting Network! We've got something like twenty new shows, and half of them star me! For instance...

...Sundays at 9:00, watch me and Cleavon Little as we play a couple of wacky cops in **MURPHY and LEEDS, HAIR-TRIGGER BLUES!**
They're cops with guns, and taking it all the way.

They've got nice clothes, a fast car, and use short sentences that don't really mean anything.

We're taking this all the way, man.

Let's do it.

When the law is not enough, it's time to call **MURPHY and LEEDS, HAIR-TRIGGER BLUES!**

So don't forget! About twenty shows, and half of them star me! Starting Sunday on the **Wally Broadcasting Network!** Catch the feeling!

The interesting thing was that out of about twenty shows, the most popular were the ones in which Cowboy Wally didn't appear.

Sure, maybe that's the way it looked on **paper**, but the truth is, there were some shows even **less** popular than the ones I starred in.

Like Rusty.

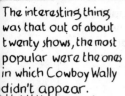

Yeah! **Nobody** liked **his** show!

But you know the media, they ignore things like that. They just want a story. But Wally's shows were much more popular than Rusty.

Rusty, 1985

The Wally Broadcasting Network
presents
THE ADVENTURES OF
RUSTY

Gramps! Rusty's trying to tell us something!

Uh, excuse me...

And now some scenes from next week's episode.

Uh, excuse me...

Gramps! Rusty's trying to tell us something!

...brought to you by--
HOWOOOOOOOOOOOOOOO
HOWOOOOOOOOOOOOOOO
HOWOOOOOOOOOOOOOOO
Dog Food.

"Dogs ask for it by name."

Medical Hospital, 1985

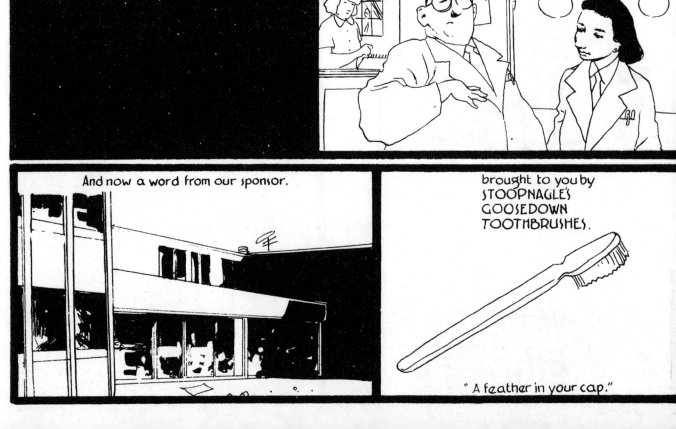

That show was a huge hit for us.

That was one of the shows you weren't in.

Yes, that was one of the shows I wasn't in!

A lot of people weren't in it.

That's right. Why don't you go pick on them.

Muckraker.

You can't ignore the fact that nobody watched the WBN shows you were in. You had lower ratings than WBN's "Charles Nelson Reilly Comedy hour."

Okay! So we canceled my shows! Happy?

Not to say that Wally didn't keep busy.

The News, 1985

Today's big story, Mayor Fenton Hubley was killed today in a tragic plane crash.

On the lighter side of the news, I never liked him anyway.

And now a word from our sponsor.

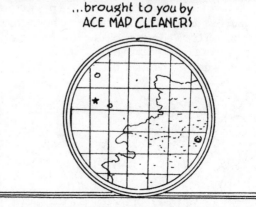

...brought to you by ACE MAP CLEANERS

"We're sweeping the nation."

Your news show was canceled a week after you took over the anchor position from Gary Morton.

It was a slow news month!

Besides, we had other things we were working on. We were launching our new children's lineup.

Oh yes. The children's shows were actually the turning point for the network.

That's right. The shows were tremendously popular, and eventually the Wally Broadcasting Network was producing children shows exclusively.

Wally wasn't in any of those shows, right?

What is it with you?

He was behind the scenes.

I was the voice of Grandpa Gloot, smart guy!

So there.

The Gloots, 1985

Hey, hey, kiddies! It's time for the adventures of America's most lovable urchins,

THE GLOOTS ™

Hello, there, you adorable little moppet, you.

Yes, we are all too cute for words.

Let us engage in antics which have made us the darlings of America.

Is it any wonder we have captured the hearts of audiences the world over?

Two guys walk into a bar, see...

...brought to you by SSENIPPAH cereal

SSENIPPAH

"Ssenippah spelled backward is happiness."

The "Al Space" program was a kind of reunion for you and ex-WQZ president Jameson Spleen.

Yes, Jameson had given me my start in show business back in '74. He had fallen on hard times in 1985, so I gave him a job playing Al Space.

I thought the show was great.

It was a strange format, though.

Yeah, just him and some kid sitting at a table for an hour every day. It was a different kid each day.

For some reason, it was a big hit.

Wally wasn't on this show, either.

That's it!

Hey! Hey!

Al Space, 1985

AL SPACE

Today, we're going to learn how to make lots of money real fast. Do you know how to make lots of money real fast, Jimmy?

Sell cigarettes at A A meetings.

Very good, Jimmy. And now for a commercial.

He loved kids. He really loved kids.

Really, really really loved kids.

A lot.

Al Space, 1985

Hey, hey, kids! It's me again! Your old pal, Al Space!

And hey! Don't forget to enter this month's Al Space **essay contest**!

In 1000 words or less, give a believable account of Al Space's whereabouts on the eve of September 15! Remember to mention that I wasn't anywhere near Wisconsin!

And now, Little Bobby Pootwaddle will read last month's contest winner.

Last month's question —
"In 1000 words or less, describe how Amy Sue Sturdfetzer looked much older than 12."

Around this time, you ran into some trouble with the FCC.

Yeah, as a sales gimmick I gave away some free commercial time.

The FCC says you ran commercials for free in order to pay off gambling debts to the mob.

Nah, that's just silly.

Al Space, 1985

Hey, kids! Don't forget to order your Al Space Decoder Ring! Only $1.99! Pretty nifty, huh, Freddy?

Mom says the reason you don't wear rings is that they would spark when you drag your knuckles on the ground.

Heh, heh... What a charming little boy. Heh, heh, heh...

Say, Freddy, do you think you can fit a nickel into that light socket over there?

...brought to you by VITO'S OLIVE OIL HEALTH TONIC.

"You'll buy it, if you want to stay healthy."

Why was Vito's Olive Oil the only company involved in your "free trial offer"?

Our free advertising gimmick was still new. Vito's was our test client.

We wanted to see if it would work before we started giving free ads to everybody.

So it wasn't a mob payoff.

What **mob**? It's a family. Vito's is a nice family business! Why do you keep saying it's a mob?

It's just a family! You've got a family yourself. We know where you live, too. So let's just forget this mob business, okay?

Deep Sea Theater, 1985

Good evening, and welcome to Deep Sea Theater.

Tonight we present the Shellfish Twins.

I'm happy as a clam.

I'm steamed.

Weren't they an unlikely pair? I sure didn't like 'em. Be here next week, when Salmon Dave sings "I'm a Sole Man." Good night.

... brought to you by
VITO'S OLIVE OIL &
VITO'S WATERPROOF
MATTRESSES

"Buy the olive oil or sleep with the fishes."

Commercial, 1986

Hi, I'm Benny Fenton! Here at Fenton's Chevrolet in Willoughbrook, we're **scalping** prices on all our 1986 cars! **Right, Wally?**

That's right, Benny. You guys at Fenton's Chevrolet in Willoughbrook sure know how to **rustle up** savings. And that's no **rope trick.** So **saddle up** and come on down to Fenton's Chevrolet in Willoughbrook and save some **buckaroos. Podner.**

COWBOY WALLY

At Fenton's Chevrolet in Willoughbrook, it's a savings roundup.

Dude!

Things were pretty bleak for you, careerwise.

Nah, I was just resting. I was making good money.

He was just waiting for the right vehicle.

How about a Chevy from Fenton's in Willoughbrook?

How about a mouthful of bloody Chiclets?

In late 1986, you found your vehicle.

That's right. I wrote and starred in my first movie.

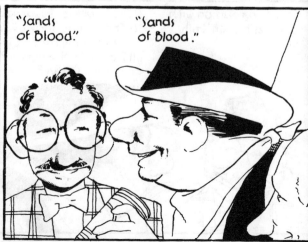

"Sands of Blood."

"Sands of Blood."

Chapter Two: Sands of Blood

Chapter Two: SANDS OF BLOOD
(Drama, 1986)

Cowboy Wally's first starring role in a motion picture and his second directorial effort (See "Ed Smith, Lizard of Doom"), **Sands of Blood** was a milestone in his career. For him, it meant a return to acting, a return to the limelight, and a return to sleeping with the kind of fabulous babes who normally wouldn't give him the time of day.

Sands of Blood was also the film that introduced the writing and acting talents of Lenny Walsh. As Stanley, the young recruit who is forced to kill twelve men, Lenny Walsh exudes a quiet intensity and the refreshing vulnerability of youth. And a vivacious alienation, too.

A hauntingly tragic, but vastly entertaining film.

Hi.

Hi, yourself. Where you going?

I'm going to France.

Right. Dumb question. Of course you're going to France. I mean, this is a boat to France. Where else **could** you be going? I mean, you're not going to jump off the boat in the middle of the Pacific Ocean! It's Atlantic. I knew that. Pacific is...

I thought you meant where am I going in France. I was just teasing you when I said, "France!" It was a joke.

I'm sorry. It's a pretty good joke now that I think about it.

Thanks. You should calm down. You seem kind of tense.

No, not really. Well, maybe. It's funny. I have a lot of trouble speaking to beautiful women. I don't know why I just said that. This isn't a pickup, you know.

Oh. Okay.

"Oh. Okay"?

What? You said "Oh. Okay". What do you mean by that? Would you like this to be a pickup? I mean if you want, it could be. I just said it's not a pickup because I thought you didn't want me to pick you up. But I could make it a pickup. If you want.

No.

Oh, then I was just kidding.

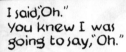

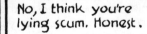

Whooshman-Bicarbonate Films presents "SANDS OF BLOOD"

Hello I'd like to join the French Foreign Legion.

Fine. We'll need your name, Social Security number, and the name of the girl you're trying to forget. That is, if you're up to it. If you're not going to start crying or anything. I know it's painful.

I'm fine. Don't worry about me.

Really? To be honest, you look like a crier to me. Don't get me wrong, now, I understand completely. I just don't want to have to look at it. Maybe we'll just do the paperwork later. Just give me your first name for now.

Stanley.

Well, hello, Stanley, and welcome to the French Foreign Legion. We congratulate you for taking this giant step toward chasing away nasty old Mr. Blues. In the years that follow, we hope you'll come to think of us here in the Legion as your friends. Have a balloon.

Thank you.

You gonna be okay? You look like you're getting kind of misty. I really don't want to have to watch that. I'll show you to your quarters now. Try not to bust out crying until we get there.

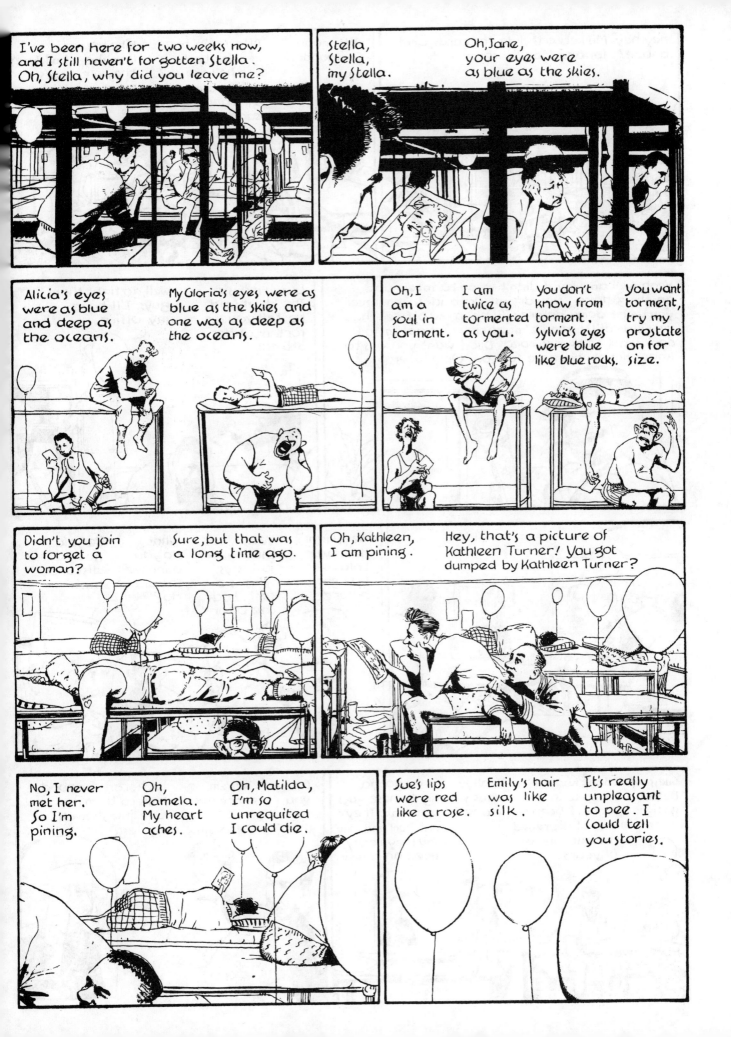

Hey, hey, Musketeers! Hide the cards and booze! *Sahara Moe is here!*

Afternoon, Commandant.

Afternoon, boys! Hey, Smitty, how the hell are ya? How's your girlfriend's eyes today? Blue?

Like the Danube they are, sir.

Sir, Madelyne's eyes were like...

Yeah, well anyway, I didn't mean to interrupt anything here, you all just go back to whatever you were doing before. I'll be in my office. The new issue of "Penthouse" magazine just got in so I don't want to be disturbed. But I want you kids to know I'm always here for you. Only later.

Excuse me, sir. The chief said to tell you the fort is under attack.

Well, go fight them, guys. I'll be in my office.

SLAM.

Gee. Fight? He never told us to fight before.

Yeah. Usually, he just says, "This is a fort. Lock the door."

What do you think we should do?

He said not to disturb him.

Guess we better go fight.

I don't know if I'm up to it today. I been kind of depressed the last couple of years.

Really? What's wrong?

So we gonna fight these guys or what? They're out front and they say they really need an answer.

Can you stall them?

Tell 'em we're not in or something.

Look, can somebody talk to them? One just shot off my leg.

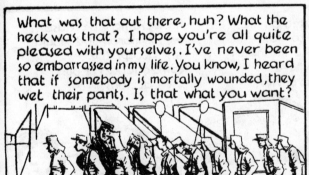

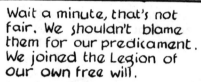

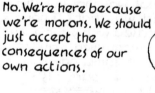

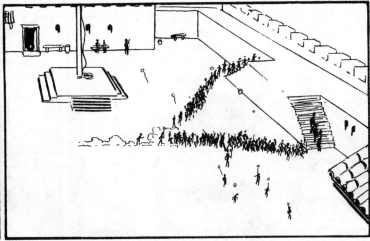

BANG BANG BANG BANG BANG BANG BANG BANG BANG BANG BANG

Die, Alice!

Eat hot lead Nina!

You're brain soup now, Pamela!

BANG BANG BANG BANGBANG BANG BANG BANG BAN

...And this is for "I'll love you forever, Harry." BANG!
...And this is for "I wish you'd trust me and open up, Harry." BANG!... And this is for "I think we should see other people, Harry." BANG!...
And this is for "We'll still be friends, Harry" BANG!

BANG BANG BANG BANG BANG BANG BANG BANG B

Hey, you, hey! Look up here! Up here!

Shoot me! Shoot me!

I'm worthless! Please kill me!

Hey! You! Hey! 'Tis a far, far better thing I do! Hey!

NG BANG BANG BANG BANG BANG BANG BANG BANG BANG BAN

Hey, Guys. Cut that out. Come on.

Why should we, Stanley? We're morons. We deserve to die.

What do we have to live for anyway, huh, Stan?

They're showing "Porky's II" on cable tonight.

Oh, okay.

BANG BANG BANG BANG BANG BANG BANG BAN

And stay down, for cryin' out loud! "Kill me, kill me, boo hoo hoo." Why, I oughta...

Gee, Stan, we'd be dead for sure if you hadn't come along.

Wow, you're a hero!

BANG BANG BANG BANG BANG BANG BANG BANG BANG

Wow,
Stanley the hero.
That must feel great.
Being a hero and
all that.

No. I'm not doing this
to be a hero. I just
don't want to see you
get kilt.

BANG BANG BANG BANG BANG BANG BANG BANG BANG

Yeah, but I'll bet you still get
kind of a rush standing there
with that gun. Bet you feel like
Clint Eastwood or something.
I know I would.

Come on,
cut it
out. I
hate
guns.

BANG BANG BANG BANG BANG BANG BANG BANG BANG BA

Yeah,
right.

No, really. I just didn't want you guys to
get hurt. I'd rather not be here,
if you want to know the truth. I don't
like fighting. I don't like guns. I don't
like killing. I don't want to be a hero.

BANG BANG BANG BANG BANG BANG BANG BANGE

Wow.

Oops. Almost
missed one.

BANG BANG BANG BANG BANG BANG BANG BANG BA

Hey, Stanley,
do you think
I could hold
the gun for
a minute, huh?

No,
you can't
hold the gun
for a minute.
Get down.

NG BANG BANG BANG BANG BANG BANG BANG BANG BANG

Come on, just for a minute.
Let me just shoot one guy,
and then I'll give it right back.

No.
Sit down.
You'll get shot.

BANG BANG BANG BANG BANG BANG BANG BANG BANG BA

Oh, okay.
I see how it is,
Mr. Rambo.

No, that's not it at all.
It's just that you'll get
killed. You want to die.

NG BANG BANG BANG BANG BANG BANG BANG BAN

No I don't. Really. That was
before. I've changed.
I'm a completely different guy
now. Rugged and manly
and stuff.

So grow
a beard.
Sit
down.

BANG BANG BANG BANG BANG BANG BANG BANG BANG B

So what do you say? Lemme get the gun for a minute, huh?

I don't know. How can I be sure? I mean, suppose you're just lying to me so I'll let you up here to kill yourself? I'd better just hold onto the gun.

NG BANG BANG BANG BANG BANG BANG BANG BANG BANG BA

You think I'd do that? You really think I'd lie to get myself killed? If I got killed right after lying, I'd go straight to Hell for sure!

What?

BANG BANG BANG BANG BANG BANG BANG BANG BANG BANG BAN

No, really! It happened to a guy in my neighborhood!

Guy in your neighborhood went to Hell.

BANG BANG BANG BANG BANG BANG BANG BANG BANG BA

Yeah, he lied to his wife about working late, and then got hit by a car and went to Hell.

How did you find out he went to Hell?

BANG BANG BANG BANG BANG BANG BANG BANG BANG B

He appeared to his son in a dream and said, "I lied to your mother, and now I'm in Hell, and boy, am I sorry!"

Right.

NG BANG BANG BANG BANG BANG BANG BANG BANG BANG BANG BAN

Really. The kid was on TV and everything! That "Sixty Minutes" show. Mike Wallace interviewed him.

I'll bet Wallace was impressed.

BANG BANG BANG BANG BANG BANG BANG BANG BANG BANG BANG B

Actually, Wallace tore him apart. Asked the kid all sorts of dumb questions to make him look bad. Stuff like "What did your father say Hell looked like?

So what did the kid say?

NG BANG BANG BANG BANG BANG BANG BANG BANG BANG BANG

He said it looked like Jackson Heights, Queens. In New York. It's all these fourteen-year-old kids wearing plaid flannel shirts over Def Leppard T-shirts. And no black people, hardly.

Probably couldn't afford the rent.

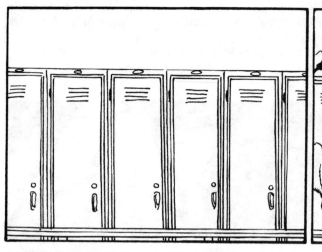

We won!
We won!

What do you mean, we? You didn't do any fighting. All you did was yell "Shoot me."

Yeah, but I didn't get shot, and they did, so we won!

If you ask me, that's a draw.

Boy, I feel great. We did it. We won the fight. You know, Hemingway was right. Killing changes a man. Makes him stronger.

You know, you do look different. Sort of a glow.

A glow?

Yeah, a glow. A manly glow.

Hey, it's Stanley! How do you feel, hero?

I murdered twelve men, and when I die, I'm going to Jackson Heights, Queens.

Hey, I just got off the phone with the President! We've got another fight lined up for tomorrow! If we keep this up, we could have a shot at the championship!

Wow, that's great, Commandant!

Hey, Charlie, what's that you're wearing?

My underwear.

Don't kid me, Charlie! You know what I mean! Is that a manly glow?

You know what we should do? We should celebrate. We should do guy stuff. Manly stuff. On account of our newfound manliness and masculinity.

So we should do guy stuff. What's guy stuff, for instance?

Like beer. We could drink beer. That's a manly thing. We could drink a lot of beer and yell "Go go go go" and "Ay ay ay ay." And belch. Belching is manly.

We could watch a sporting event while drinking beer.

I want to spit and swear and adjust my shorts on a street corner. That would be guy stuff. Can we do that?

Hey, let's drive around and yell out of car windows at women.

And drink beer.

And drink beer.

Hey, Stanley! Want to do guy stuff?

Sure! We'll go!

Jeez, you mean you're gonna bring your wimp friends with you? Holy crap. They'll ruin everything.

We're not wimps, we're just sensitive.

Yeah, sensitive.

Whatever. I don't think you should be allowed to do guy stuff.

How come?

Yeah, how come?

Because you shouldn't, that's why. Because... because you didn't kill anybody. You didn't kill anybody, so now you shouldn't be allowed to do guy stuff. Sure, that makes sense, doesn't it? Stanley can come, because he's a hero. He killed a bunch of guys.

I was gonna kill some people. I was working up to it.

Well, here we are. A hardy band of Legionnaires out for a night on the town.

We're glad you could come along, Commandant.

You kidding? To watch you do guy stuff, I'd miss my own funeral.

Thanks for letting us come along, too.

What letting? You followed us.

Of course we followed you. We thought we were invited.

That's why you followed us with the lights off. That's why you waited around the corner while we got gas. That's why you spent most of the trip disguised as old ladies.

So, what're you saying?

Hey, come on. I want to do guy stuff! What are we gonna do first?

How 'bout we go into this bar and knock back a few Brewskis.

And arm wrestle.

Yahoo! Let's go!

I'll be along in a minute. I want to swear and spit awhile out here first.

Something wrong, Ike?

No, it's just that, well, what if somebody asks me, "See the game last night?" If I tell them I didn't, they'll think I'm a fag or something.

So say you saw it.

What if they quiz me?

So, what do you do?

We're coat-check girls.

Oh, really?

No, we just said that to impress you.

Blanche, that wasn't nice.

That's okay, it was a pretty good joke.

I'm sorry. I don't know what's the matter with me. I shouldn't pick on you. You seem like a nice guy. I mean, you've got it bad enough as it is, without me picking on you.

What do you mean?

It's just an awkward situation. You're trying to pick Fifi up, but you don't want to offend her friend, namely me. So you're being a good sport and talking to both of us, even though you really just want to talk to Fifi.

You probably also hate yourself for the fact that you're more attracted to Fifi than to me. You think it's wrong to prefer Fifi just on the basis of her looks, but at the same time you can't help yourself. You suspect that I may secretly be jealous of Fifi because men usually ask her out and not me.

You're probably thinking about asking me out because you feel sorry for me. Or because you feel guilty. But you really want Fifi. She's so beautiful. The kind of girl every guy wants. Every guy. She probably has zillions of guys. Big guys. Rich guys. Most likely, she wouldn't go out with you. You think maybe you'd have better luck with me because I'm less attractive. Yep, it's an awkward situation all right.

I hear you're coat-check girls. That sounds like interesting work.

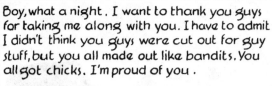

Boy, what a night. I want to thank you guys for taking me along with you. I have to admit I didn't think you guys were cut out for guy stuff, but you all made out like bandits. You all got chicks. I'm proud of you.

Wasn't nothing, boss. Chicks are impressed by rugged killers.

You didn't kill anybody.

That's beside the point. The chicks thought I did.

So we'll kill some people next time around.

Right.

Stanley the hero got two chicks last night. They bought him drinks.

They said I seemed so "pathetic."

Don't knock it. The pity angle is just as valid as any other pickup technique.

I guess.

What do you mean, you "guess"? Two chicks, Stanley! Two chicks fell for that "helpless little boy" routine last night! What more do you want!

Would you have been happier if you had been able to go up to some girl and give her some slick line? If she had then giggled and batted her eyes and tossed her hair around? Would you have been happy then? Do you really want some ditzy chick who would fall like a sack of warm marshmallows for some phony line?

You mean chicks like you guys got?

You think we're happy?

Did you ever notice that most really beautiful women never seem to have anything worthwhile to say?

You mean that the prettiest girls are also the dizziest? Yes, I have noticed that.

It's just really annoying. I mean, sure they're beautiful and all that, but they're lousy to talk to. I'm never interested in the crap they talk about.

I wouldn't mind having a really beautiful girlfriend, though. I wish I could just tell her, right off, before we get involved, "Look, you're beautiful and all that, I'll give you presents, take you dancing, buy you dinner, make love to you, do anything you want, give you anything you want, I'll treat you like a queen, for chrissakes, but if you try to talk to me, I'll break your arm."

Sounds like a great deal. If I were a beautiful woman, I'd take it.

I don't know, though. Every beautiful woman can't be an idiot. It's not possible, is it? I mean, it can't be a genetic thing. Maybe they're just faking it. Maybe they think guys like girls who act ditzy and helpless.

Get outta here. You're crazy. Why would a girl act stupid if she really weren't?

Why did we all put on the macho soldier act?

But we really **are** soldiers!

But we're not as cool and manly as we pretend to be. Look at us right now. We're the goddamn whiner brigade!

Yeah, but women like manly men, not whiners.

Stanley got two women.

Thanks loads.

Sure he got two women. Stanley's a nice guy. We're all nice guys. We just don't have faith in our own appeal and so we put on acts.

Damn straight, I put on an act. If I don't put on an act, I'll just be a normal guy. There's nothing special about me.

So be a normal guy, for Chrissakes! It'll make you stand out from the crowd. There aren't too many normal guys around anymore. Everybody's got an act. Some are better than others, but they're still acts. Deep down, everybody's the same, anyway. All anyone wants is to be loved. That goes for women as well as men.

Wow, that's beautiful. I'm touched. I really am. I'd cry, but it makes me look like Oprah Winfrey Look, I hate to break up this rap session, but we've got a fight scheduled in fifteen minutes and I want you all to get showered.

Fight?

Yeah, remember? I told you guys yesterday.

Commandant, enemy sighted on the horizon. They should be here in a minute.

But sir, we can't fight.

Damn. They're ten minutes early.

Sir, Murphy's on cannons. He said to ask you if we have any of the good cannonballs left.

What do you mean, you can't fight?

Sir? We've kind of got a situation out here. We really need to know about those cannonballs.

We can't fight them, they're soldiers like us. Maybe they have the same problems we have.

Yeah.

I doubt it. I can hardly believe that **you** have the problems you have.

Sir, Murphy says— Oh, never mind. They got Murphy sir.

We're sorry, sir, but it's how we feel.

Oh, this is great, just great. We're dead men. I wish you guys had told me about this earlier. I would have had time to sneak out the back.

Can I come in, sir? I have to go to the bathroom.

This sucks. This really sucks. I hope you know that.

I'm sorry, sir, we can't fight them. It would be wrong.

We're dead men. This really, really sucks, guys.

Come on, let me in, sir, please.

Maybe if we surrender, they won't kill us.

I'd rather die.

You're in luck, sir. They'd rather kill us.

We could kill ourselves.

That's brilliant.

I wonder what it'll be like, being dead.

Do you believe in God, sir?

I did until about 30 seconds ago. Now if you'll excuse me, I figure I've got about two minutes left to get stinking drunk.
It's sad, really. We could have done so much together. Don't you see? We weren't just fighting men, we were defending a way of life!

Making the world a safer place for our children and ensuring the rights of every freedom-loving man and woman! And now we're throwing it all away. Can you do that? Can you sit back and watch our precious way of life be destroyed by these monsters? Can you? No! You'll fight! Fight like lions! Fight because you must! Fight for what's just!

Wait a minute. Sometimes I'm so dumb I could puke. This is a fort! Lock the door.

the
end

a cowboy wally production

Sands of Blood
Produced by Cowboy Wally
directed by Cowboy Wally
Written by Lenny Walsh with
    Cowboy Wally.

Cast
Sahara Moe   Cowboy Wally
Stanley   Lenny Walsh
Charlie   Knees McCullough
Ike   JoJo Walker
George   Stretch Armstrong
Big Harry   The McPiffle Sisters
Manny
Moe   } The Pep Boys
Jack
Fifi   Ilene Loeb of "Ilene Loeb
                  and her Singing Tuba"
and Charles Du Gaulle as himself

Key Grip   Who cares.

Watch for the upcoming films
"Sands of Blood Bloopers," and
"Sands of Blood Bloopers 2."

© 1986 Cowboy Wally Entertainment

A Whooshman-Bicarbonate Film.

Chapter Three: THE MAKING OF
"HAMLET"
(documentary, 1986)

One of Cowboy Wally's forgotten classics, his greatly improved version of Shakespeare's popular tragedy has been largely ignored by critics and film historians. Recently rediscovered, it remains as avant-garde as ever.

The Making of Hamlet is the filmed diary of a genius in the act of creation. We follow Cowboy Wally as he brings his grand vision to life. In a bold move which sends murmurs of indignation rippling throughout the motion-picture and dramatic-arts communities, he rewrites the play completely and shortens it to twenty minutes.

This film failed miserably at the box office, once again proving Cowboy Wally to be a progressive visionary and ahead of his time.

Hey, hey, folks! It's me, your old pal Cowboy Wally! I thought some of you might be curious about what goes on during an average day here at Cowboy Wally Entertainment, Inc. Or, more importantly, what it's like to be Cowboy Wally.

New York, 1987

So what I decided to do was make this movie. I don't know what the title is going to be yet, maybe "A day in the life" or something...

...I'll worry about it later, after I get the film back and put it all together. But what I'm going to do is, see, I've set up cameras around the room and now I'm going to go to my desk and work, and act like there's no cameras filming me. Okay? This should be fun.

I love making movies. My most recent film, **Sands of Blood** was just released today. As a matter of fact, Chester just went out to get a newspaper, so I can read the review.

Chester used to be vice-president of Warner Brothers, but now he's the janitor here at CWE. We kid him about it.

Chester says that there's just as much dignity in being a janitor as there is in being vice-president of Warner Brothers. He's always saying funny things like that. He should be a stand-up comedian. He's a riot.

Actually, he really does want to be a comedian. What he needs is for somebody in show business to give him his big break.

Anyway, let's get this movie started, okay?

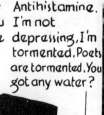

There he is, fellows! Cowboy Wally!

What's with the camera?

Lenny Walsh, I want you to meet the heads of Whooshman-Bicarbonate Films, Mr. Hib Whooshman, and Mr. Harrison Bicarbonate. Sol here yet?

No, he's not coming. Great to meet you, Lenny. I love the kind of crazy stuff you're doing. I think it's just terrific. I hear Rex called it a "tearjerker."

What do you mean, Sol's not coming? I told him to be here.

We called him and told him he didn't have to come.

What do you mean? He's my manager!

We just figured we didn't need him at this meeting.

Come on, everything's fine. Don't worry about it. Sit down. Have a drink.

Yeah, Okay.

What did you say the camera was for?

In case my manager didn't show up.

Oh.

So, uh, anyway, let's get down to business. Basically, we loved the work you guys did on "Sands of Blood," and we want another movie from you.

Sure, we can work something up for you, right, Len?

Oh, yeah. Sure.

Great. We're real enthusiastic about it. Sounds great.

We're giving you a budget of 10 million. The thing is, for tax reasons we need this movie by the end of the fiscal year.

Sure. When's that?

Next Friday.

We got scripts! You need scripts?

A movie by next Friday! Sounds great! What kind scripts you got?

We got some really fantastic scripts by some new kids on the coast. They're really out of this world. We've got one called "Dead to Rights," about a he-man killing machine for hire.

He's two-fisted.

Sounds great!

It is great. The script needs a lot of rewrites, but it's a great title. And we came up with a great line for the poster.

Yeah. Get this. We have a picture of this guy, with guns and stuff all over him and underneath we have the line, "He's through running. Now it's his turn."

That's great!

What's it mean?

I think we can get Bruce Willis. Whaddaya say?

We got other scripts. We got lotsa scripts.

Let's do "Hamlet."

Shakespeare, right?

I don't know, Len...

Lenny's kidding. He's a riot. HAW!

"They killed his father. Now he's fighting back. When the law is not enough, it's time to call Hamlet."

That could work.

Is he two-fisted? We'll do it if he's two-fisted!

Hamlet?

Sure!

Sounds fabulous! For one thing, it's not copyrighted.

And it's violent! We'll do it!

I just remembered. Lenny and I have to make a call.

To who?

To who?

Your old grand-dad. Phone's by the bar.

Great idea.

"HAMLET"?   I was kidding.

Too bad. They love the idea. Now we have to do it. Balls.

Could be worse. After all, it is one of the greatest plays ever written.

Yeah, right. I know the kind of plays you think are "great". The guy dies at the end, right?

Yeah. So?

I figured.   Anytime somebody writes a play where the guy dies at the end, it's a masterpiece.   Any sex?

What?

Is there any sex in "Hamlet"?

No, of course not.

Right. No sex, guy dies. Great play.

Give me another drink, Lucille. Hey, Lucille, you like "Hamlet"?

I can't remember. I read it in high school. Why?

It's our next movie.

Oh, really? How come?

Because Lenny's a jerk.

Come on, "Hamlet"'s a masterpiece.

Masterpiece, hm? What, does he die at the end or somethin'?

Len, we've only just met, so I don't know you too well...

Call me Len.

Len, I don't know you too well, so correct me if I'm wrong... but you seem kind of cranky.

I'm not cranky. Babies are cranky. Old men are cranky. I'm tormented.

I don't think old men are cranky so much as grumpy. Old men are grumpy.

I'm sleepy, dopey, and happy.

I'm sneezy.

From a chest cold?

You know what's good for that? Vicks'.

What are you, running a business on the side? Local distributor of Vicks'?

Sue me. I like Vicks'!

So I hear!

Cranky, like I said before. Cranky.

You were right in the first place. You should have stuck with it. Cranky.

Tormented! I'm tormented!

What about, for Pete's sake!?

He gets like that when he's cranky.

I hate you. I really hate you.

See that? Rex Reed calls him a "tearjerker," and all of a sudden, he's a temperamental genius. Look, he's already forgetting his friends.

Well, anyway back to "Hamlet"...

This isn't "Hamlet"! It's a joke!

What do you mean?

Ask Vanna White.

You know Vanna White?

Could you talk to her for us?

I don't know Vanna White!

Then what are you talking about?

I'm talking about the way you're destroying one of the greatest plays ever written!

What destroying? We're making it better!

Lenny, we're not destroying anything. The story of "Hamlet" was around for years before Shakespeare even got to it!

Sure, Len, just because something's old doesn't mean it's engraved in stone. We know a lot more about entertainment now than they did back then.

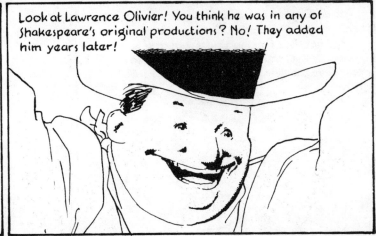

Look at Lawrence Olivier! You think he was in any of Shakespeare's original productions? No! They added him years later!

Gee, Wally, I guess you're right.

Great! Fantastic. Look, Harrison and I have to go now, but you're welcome to stay here and have a couple of drinks on us.

Thanks! Aw, jeez, I just drank Lenny's drink by mistake. Now I'm gonna get your cold.

Here, you better take some of these.

Okay, see you later, then. Get to work, you tearjerkers, you.

Hey, hey, folks! It's your old pal, Cowboy Wally! And I gotta tell you what just happened.

Okay, this is really funny. See, after we left Lucille's... Oh, right, remember we were at 'Lucille's'. Well, that was yesterday...

...This is today's film. So anyway, right, we walk out of Lucille's, the restaurant, and so I say to Lenny, I say to him...

...Wait. Okay, so first, we're at Lucille's, and Hib Whooshman and Harrison Bicarbonate leave, and so Lenny and I stick around and have some drinks. They said we could, Hib and Harrison, and they said to charge it to them.

...So anyway, we had some drinks, and so we walk out of Lucille's and... Oh, right, wait, Lenny has like five more scotches and he's taking these cough pills and syrup and so we leave Lucille's, and Lenny's being real cranky...

Cranky, cranky, cranky.

So I say to Lenny, I say, "Hey, Lenny..." No, wait, Lenny says to me, he says, no, this guy, this guy comes up to me, and he says, "You have the right to remain silent..."

Wait. There's a jump there somewhere...

045-78901

So anyway, hey, hey, kids! It's your old pal, Cowboy Wally! Today, we're here at the Ryker's Island State Correctional facility in New York.

I'm here with my buddy Lenny, and on the other side of the glass are my manager, Sol, and my lawyer, Carmine! And, of course, you all know my cameraman.

How'm I doin', guys? When do I get out of here?

Okay, I just got through talking to the judge about your case. I told him just what you said to. I go to the judge and I say "The evidence against my clients is circumstantial, and those girls brought their own drugs and Wally and Lenny didn't know it was a Laundromat, and the pony was there when they arrived."

Perfect. You did good.

Well, see, that's the thing. The judge says you guys were arrested for urinating in an alley. That's just a hundred-dollar fine.

Great! So all we have to do is pay the hundred, and I'm out of here.

Not anymore. Now the judge is curious about this Laundromat thing. They're holding you guys here pending an investigation.

No! They can't do that!

Say guys, can I go home? I mean, I wasn't involved in any of this last night, I couldn't have been. I'm pretty sure I was unconscious at the time.

Are you kidding? You drove the car!

Impossible. I don't know how to drive.

I know. It was a riot.

Sorry I missed it.

Lenny, how can you be so selfish? Why do you hate the common man so? Why do you want to deprive them of the cultural advantages you have?

I know your kind. You like the idea that Shakespeare belongs to a select group of intellectuals. You like the fact that you can quote Shakespeare at a party, and only one or two people will really know what you're talking about. Shakespeare is the secret language of an intellectual in-crowd. Your secret club. With your secret club code.

You don't appreciate Shakespeare. Shakespeare was an entertainer. You're just using his genius to make yourself feel superior to other people. If anyone has destroyed Shakespeare's work, it's you.

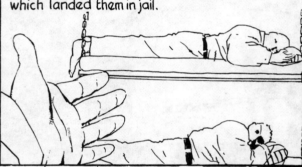

And what about these guys? Our cellmates. This movie may be their only chance at a decent life! Look at them. Products of broken homes, hard luck, poverty. Driven to lives of crime, which landed them in jail.

When they get out of here, nobody will hire them. They'll be forced to return to crime. Society has turned it's back on them. These guys will never get a decent break. We're the only chance these guys have left.

I say, we're the only chance these guys have left.

OH! AAAAGH AAAAAAGH OH!

Hey! Hey! Wake up! You were having a nightmare!

Oh, it was awful! I was drowning! Drowning in a sea of hopelessness! Alone.

There, there. Everything's going to be all right.

Will it? Will it really? I so want to believe that...

Okay, okay. I'll do it.

Hey, 'Cisco!

Freeze, dirtbag!

Open sesame, for Chrissakes! It's Horatio and Marcellus!

Oh, hey. I'm sorry.

Calm down, man. You're gonna kill somebody if you don't watch it.

You're right. You're right. I don't know what's wrong with me. I'm just a bundle of nerves.

Anyway, we were in the neighborhood, and--

Hey! Hey! Who's that?

Relax, Francisco. It's just the King's ghost.

Sorry. I didn't recognize him. He's been here three nights in a row.

What does he want?

I don't know. He just stands there, staring. It's really bothering me.

Well, ask him what he wants!

Can we do that? I mean, you're not supposed to talk to the King without first being spoken to.

But he's a ghost now. Maybe ghosts have to wait for us.

Hey, he's opening his mouth. He's going to speak!

COCK-A-DOODLE-DOO!

Hey, he disappeared!

Who? I didn't see any ghost of a king who died suspiciously. Did you?

Can't we just use a cutout for Ophelia?

Lenny! He was just kidding! He doesn't want to jeopardize his only shot at a decent life!

Yeah, I guess I'm just being silly.

Of course you are! It was just a joke!

Actually, I thought this was some kind of casting couch thing.

Hey, here comes Maxine!

Hide the camera behind the bunks! But keep filming! Get those costumes off!

Hey, Maxine.

Hey, guys. What's new?

Not much. Got a letter from my mother.

That's nice.

I miss her very much. She's a wonderful woman. This is all probably very hard on her. You have any children?

Oh, yes. They're all grown up, though. I don't hear from them much. It's nice that you keep in touch.

Could you do me a favor? Could you read this letter to me? I'd like to hear a woman's voice reading it.

Sure, I understand. "Dear Hamlet".. Hamlet?

Nickname.

Oh. That's nice. "Dear Hamlet..."

Boy, am I glad they're gone. They give me the creeps. There's definitely something funny going on around here.

Maybe they're right. I've got to stop dwelling on this. I need something to take my mind off my troubles. I think I'll try to kill myself again.

No, that's crazy. Maybe I'm having a nervous breakdown. I'm angry all the time. I should throw something. Break something. But this is all my mother's stuff. I can't break any of this stuff. I'll go to my room and break something there. No, I can't break any of that stuff. I'd have to replace it.

This stinks. I want to break **something**, for Pete's sake. I'm all angry and tense and no way to let it out.

I've got to calm down. I'll have a drink. Then I'll be calm and I'll be able to think. Everything's going to be all right.

Hey, Hamlet!

Horatio! My best buddy! Sit down! Have a drink with me. I need to talk to somebody.

Yeah, okay. Look, Hamlet, I have to talk to you. I'm worried about your father.

I know what you mean. There's something funny about the way he died.

Not only that, but he's been pestering the guards.

What? I mean, he's not really doing anything, just staring. But it's really awkward. I never know what to say to the guy. You don't want to mention the gaping wounds, but if you talk about the weather or sports, he'll know you're just trying not to mention the gaping wounds!

Well, so long, Ophelia, my sister. My ship sails in an hour. Take care of yourself until I get back. Don't do anything I wouldn't do.

Act I
Scene III

Like what?

Like sleeping with that nut, Hamlet!

He's not a nut, he's a perfect gentleman.

Yeah, whatever. I just hear you been spendin' a lot of time with him. Just make sure he doesn't try to get anything off you.

He's been very gallant and civilized on our dates. We're even going on a picnic tomorrow.

Well, be careful. He's tricky. First it's a picnic, next thing you know, you're climbing Mount Baldy.

Hey, don't be vulgar in front of your sister, boy.

Hi, Dad, I was just leaving.

That's a good idea. So, Ophelia, what were you guys talking about?

Hamlet. We've been going out.

He get anything off you?

No He's a nice boy!

It's always the nice boys you gotta watch out for. They act real polite, tip their hats, give you flowers. Next thing you know, you're polishing Flipper.

Dad, is it true you were abandoned in the woods and raised by truckers?

Hey, don't look at me. I read it in "Cosmo"!

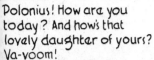

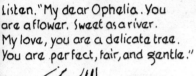

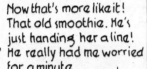

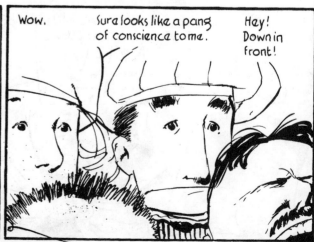

Chapter Four: Cowboy Wally's Late Night Celebrity Showdown.

Chapter Four: COWBOY WALLY'S LATE NIGHT CELEBRITY SHOWDOWN (TV show, 1987)

Special repeat presentation of one of the most requested episodes of the popular late-night talk show.

Cowboy Wally and his guest, actress Linda Mason, are joined by former announcer Eddie Foy and old-time singing cowboy Skeets Palomino for a night of memories, anecdotes, and small-arms fire.

This single episode increased the ratings of the show to such a degree that the following episodes were shown without commercials because no one could afford the advertising rates. The show was canceled two weeks later.

Hey, hey, kids! From New York, it's Cowboy Wally's Late Night Celebrity Showdown!

And here's your host, Cowboy Wally!

CLAP CLAP CLAP CLAP CLAP CLAP CLAP CLAP CLAP CLAP CLAP CLAP C Thank you, thank you. Well, we've got a really great show for you tonight. Our guests are actress Linda Mason, old-time singing cowboy Skeets Palomino, and Mason Spoon, faith healer from Mars. Plus our regular features.

But first, let me introduce the band! Our bandleader, "Toots" Walsh.

CLAP CLAP CLAP CLAP CLAP CLAP CLAP CLAP CLAP CL
Thanks, Wally. It's always great to be here. Hey, "Toots" you see today's "National Enquirer"? There's a guy who claims that space aliens turned him into a raincoat.

Really? What'd he do?

Nothing. It was reversible.

Anyway, we'll be back after this message.

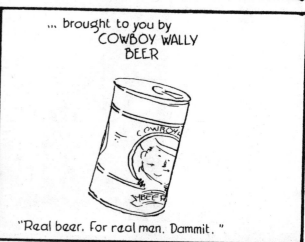

... brought to you by
COWBOY WALLY
BEER

"Real beer. For real men. Dammit."

Hi, folks. We're back! Our first guest is a very talented and acclaimed actress. She's starred in such films as "The Mother Teresa Story" and starred in "Streetcar Named Desire" and "Long Day's Journey Into Night" on Broadway. She's also on the covers of "Time," "People," and "Life" this week.

So let's have a big welcome for Linda Mason! CLAPCLAPCLAPCLAP CLAPCLAP CLAPCLAP CLAPCLAPCLAP CL

Thanks, it's wonderful to be here. I'm a big fan of yours.

Thank you!

I especially liked "Sands of Blood." Through the story of twenty lonely men, you illuminated the plight of women everywhere.

Yeah, well, you know I'm all for the plight and suffrage of women.

I think you're great. The way you lampoon outdated sexual stereotypes and other Hollywood conventions. I think you're brilliant.

Thank you very much. You've got a new movie coming out.

Yes, it's called "No Jury Would." I play a lawyer defending a man who has been wrongly accused of murder.

Sounds great. I hear you wear a bathing suit at the end.

Isn't he great, folks? The way he satirizes the mentality of the motion picture industry?

You've brought a film clip.

Yes, this is the scene where CIA agents try to kill my client.

Well, we're not going to show that, because I want to show a clip from your 1981 classic "Rita Merkel, Leather Barbarian Girl."

Rita! The Polar Huns are approaching! There are thousands of them! We must surrender the map of Zon!

No! We must never surrender the map!

Never! Even if it means that I will be captured, tied up, stripped, dipped in oil, and forced to wrestle the Polar Hun Queen in 3-D, we must never surrender!

Oh, man, I'm so embarrassed.

That was great! I've always liked that movie!

Really? I guess you would! It was a "camp" film. We wanted to lampoon the film industry. It's a lot like what you're doing.

I liked it because you kept falling down, so we could see up your skirt.

You noticed that? That was actually my idea. I wanted to say something about sexism in movies, you know?

Well, it was very effective. I own a videotape of that movie, and I like to watch those parts in slow motion.

Hahaha. You're so funny. You really are. I love that thing you do with the beer.

Really? What thing with the beer?

When you drink a whole lot of it! How do you come up with ideas like that?

Speaking of beer, we'll be right back after this message.

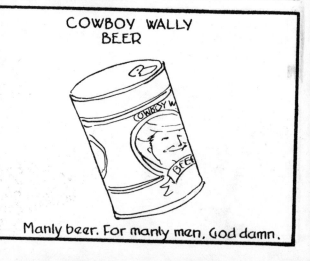

COWBOY WALLY BEER

Manly beer. For manly men, God damn.

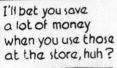

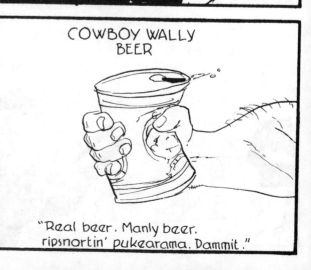

COWBOY WALLY
BEER

"Real beer. Manly beer. ripsnortin' pukearama. Dammit."

Ladies and gentlemen, old time singing cowboy Skeets Palomino is with us here tonight to amuse us with anecdotes from television's Golden Age!

I was just ribbing Skeets before, because we actually have a past experience in common. Remember, Skeets?

How could I forget, Wally?

How could I forget a young boy named Wally who auditioned for my show back in 1964? A starry-eyed youngster who wanted to be on TV. He sang "Mammy" for me.

Yeah, yeah, tell 'em what you said.

I told him that he had no talent and he would never make it in show business.

Hee, hee, I remember, I was so mad, I went out and slandered you! I ruined your career!

Boy, I was a nutty kid back then, huh? You were furious! You swore you would get me if it was the last thing you did!

Which brings us to why I'm here...

See? This is the kind of thing I was talking about!

Shut up! You had your turn! Besides, I was young then! It doesn't count!

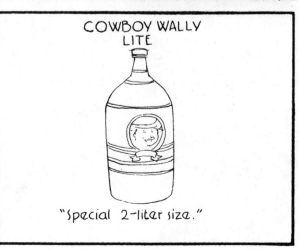

COWBOY WALLY LITE

"Special 2-liter size."

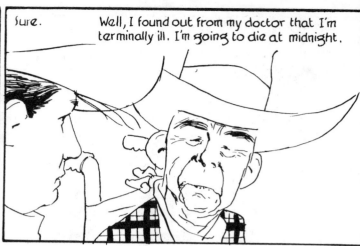

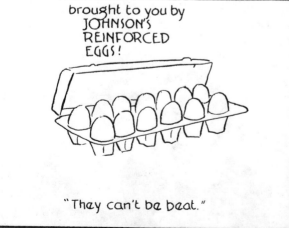

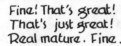
Fine! That's great!
That's just great!
Real mature. Fine.

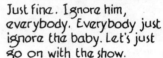
Just fine. Ignore him,
everybody. Everybody just
ignore the baby. Let's just
go on with the show.

What.

I don't know.
It's just...

What! What'd I do! How come I'm the
bad guy! I didn't do anything!

I guess you're right. It's just that you were hitting that
corpse— Of course, he wasn't really dead, but— Well, I want
to believe you're an okay guy and all, but if all these
people hate you so much, maybe— I don't know. Like the
slander thing— But you were young, maybe you've changed.

I just don't know what to think. I like
you, but maybe these guys are right
about you. I just don't know.
I wish I didn't admire you so.

It's
a
skit.

Epilogue

the
end

Special thanks to Edwin Baker, Joe Dator, Dwayne Turner, and Valerie Weber.